rib-tickl SPELLING

Strengthening Basic Skills with Jokes, Comics, and Riddles

GRADE 4

by Darcy Andries

Carson-Dellosa Publishing Company, Inc.
Greensboro, North Carolina

Credits

Content Editors: Elizabeth Swenson and Ashley Anderson

Copy Editors: Denise McAllister and Barrie Hoople

Layout and Cover Design: Nick Greenwood

Inside Illustrations: Chris Sabatino, Robbie Short, Nick Greenwood, and Christian Elden

Cover Illustration: Nick Greenwood

This book has been correlated to state, national, and Canadian provincial standards. Visit *www.carsondellosa.com* to search for and view its correlations to your standards.

ISBN 978-1-93602-217-5

Table of Contents

Page Number	Compound Words & Contractions	Consonants, Digraphs & Silent Letters	Root Words, Prefixes & Suffixes	Syllables	Vowels	Word Endings & Plurals	Word Study
5					●		
6					●		
7					●		
8					●		
9					●		
10					●		
11					●		
12					●		
13					●		
14					●		
15					●		
16					●		
17					●		
18					●		
19					●		
20					●		
21					●		
22					●		
23		●					
24		●					
25		●					
26		●					
27		●					
28		●					
29						●	
30						●	
31						●	
32		●					
33		●					
34		●					
35		●					
36		●					
37		●					
38						●	
39						●	

Page Number	Compound Words & Contractions	Consonants, Digraphs & Silent Letters	Root Words, Prefixes & Suffixes	Syllables	Vowels	Word Endings & Plurals	Word Study
40						●	
41	●						
42	●						
43				●			
44				●			
45				●			
46							●
47							●
48							●
49			●				
50			●				
51			●				
52			●				
53			●				
54			●				
55			●				
56			●				
57			●				
58			●				
59			●				
60			●				
61			●				
62			●				
63			●				
64			●				
65			●				
66			●				
67							●
68							●
69	●						
70							●
71							●
72							●
73							●
74							●

Runaway Banana

Write the word for each clue. Then, match the symbols in the answers to the symbols below. To solve the riddle, write the correct letters on the lines.

after	fabric
facts	glass
past	plant
ranch	snack
stamp	

What do you **call** a runaway banana?

1. a type of farm that usually has cattle ____ ____ ____ ____ ____
                                                      ☆

2. another word for *cloth* ____ ____ ____ ____ ____ ____
                                      ☉   □

3. to place seeds in the ground ____ ____ ____ ____ ____
                                                △

4. what can be eaten between meals ____ ____ ____ ____ ____

5. the opposite of *future* ____ ____ ____ ____
                              ⦚

6. the opposite of *opinions* ____ ____ ____ ____ ____
                                              ✓

7. what is placed on an envelope ____ ____ ____ ____ ____
                                   ↗

8. the clear part of a window ____ ____ ____ ____ ____
                                        ○

9. the opposite of *before* ____ ____ ____ ____ ____

Answer:

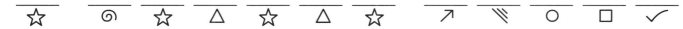

____ ____ ____ ____ ____ ____ ____ ____ ____ ____ ____ ____
 ☆   ☉   ☆   △   ☆   △   ☆   ↗   ⦚   ○   □   ✓

Chicken Garden

Write the word for each clue. To solve the riddle, match the answers to the words in the word bank. Then, write the underlined letters in order on the lines below.

breakfast   extra

feather   fresh

healthy   hedge

never   pledge

spelling

What does a chicken grow in her **garden**?

1. the opposite of *old* or *stale* _____

2. putting letters in the correct order to form words _____

3. a row of bushes that serves as a fence _____

4. a promise _____

5. the opposite of *sick* _____

6. more than necessary _____

7. the opposite of *always* _____

8. a part of a bird's wing _____

9. a morning meal _____

Answer:

Name _____

Chips and Dip

Write the mirror image of each word.

1. package _____

2. middle _____

3. prints _____

4. myth _____

5. pinch _____

6. typical _____

7. fiction _____

8. building _____

9. village _____

10. gym _____

11. built _____

12. wreckage _____

Crack the Code

Use the code to write each word.

Code:	M	N	O	P	Q	R	S	T	U	V	W	X	Y
Letter:	a	b	c	d	e	f	g	h	i	j	k	l	m

Code:	Z	A	B	C	D	E	F	G	H	I	J	K	L
Letter:	n	o	p	q	r	s	t	u	v	w	x	y	z

1. ___ ___ ___ ___ ___
   O   T   A   Y   B

2. ___ ___ ___ ___
   I   M   E   T

3. ___ ___ ___ ___ ___ ___
   E   F   D   A   Z   S

4. ___ ___ ___ ___ ___ ___
   B   A   O   W   Q   F

5. ___ ___ ___ ___ ___
   Z   A   H   Q   X

6. ___ ___ ___ ___ ___
   I   M   F   O   T

7. ___ ___ ___ ___ ___
   E   A   X   H   Q

8. ___ ___ ___ ___
   P   D   A   B

9. ___ ___ ___ ___
   R   D   A   S

10. ___ ___ ___ ___ ___
    E   T   A   O   W

11. ___ ___ ___ ___ ___
    D   A   N   U   Z

12. ___ ___ ___ ___ ___ ___ ___
    B   D   A   N   X   Q   Y

Buttons

Write the word for each clue. Then, match the symbols in the answers to the symbols below. To solve the riddle, write the correct letters on the lines.

brother	bucket
front	funny
nothing	puppet
skunk	slug

*What kind of **button** will not **unbutton**?*

1. a toy that fits on the hand   __ __ __ __ __ __
   ♡

2. another word for *pail*   __ __ __ __ __ __
   ☐

3. a black and white animal   __ __ __ __ __
   △

4. the opposite of *back*   __ __ __ __ __
   ○

5. a male sibling   __ __ __ __ __ __ __
   ☺

6. something that makes you laugh is   __ __ __ __ __
   ⇨

7. the opposite of *everything*   __ __ __ __ __ __ __
   ◇

8. an insect without a shell   __ __ __ __
   ◉

Answer:

a ___ ___ ___ ___ ___   ___ ___ ___ ___ ___ ___
  ☺ ♡ ◉ ◉ ⇨   ☺ ☐ ◇ ◇ ○ △

Making the Grade

Look at each pronunciation. Write two words that sound like each pronunciation but are spelled differently.

1. /stāk/ _____ _____

2. /rāz/ _____ _____

3. /wā/ _____ _____

4. /wāt/ _____ _____

5. /āt/ _____ _____

6. /wāst/ _____ _____

7. /pān/ _____ _____

8. /grāt/ _____ _____

9. /brāk/ _____ _____

10. /pāl/ _____ _____

Surfing Lion

What **kind** of lion likes to surf?

A sea **lion**!

Circle the words in the puzzle.

blind	bright	cried	flies	giant
high	idea	knife	mice	mighty
shyness	stripe	tie	trying	why

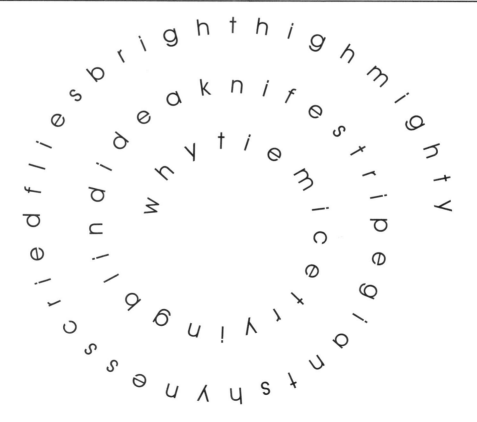

Balancing Act

Unscramble each word. Then, complete the crossword puzzle.

edlif   _____

peches   _____

efed   _____

adbe   _____

aedrm   _____

yrsot   _____

eicfh   _____

retsec   _____

nsuyn   _____

raebz   _____

That Crow Can't Go!

Can you name a type of **crow** that cannot fly?

Circle each correctly spelled word and write it on the line. To solve the riddle, write the underlined letters from the circled words in order on the lines below.

1. fl<u>o</u>et   flo<u>a</u>t   _____

2. <u>g</u>os   goe<u>s</u>   _____

3. coec<u>h</u>   <u>c</u>oach   _____

4. al<u>m</u>oust   <u>a</u>lmost   _____

5. th<u>r</u>own   thro<u>a</u>n   _____

6. po<u>e</u>m   p<u>o</u>am   _____

7. ohce<u>a</u>n   o<u>c</u>ean   _____

8. <u>r</u>oses   roe<u>s</u>es   _____

9. al<u>o</u>ne   al<u>o</u>wn   _____

10. shallo<u>w</u>   s<u>h</u>alloh   _____

Answer:

____ ____ ____ ____ ____ ____ ____ ____ ____ ____

What's Cooking?

Write the correct spelling of each word.

1. spair _____

2. everyware _____

3. repare _____

4. declair _____

5. upstares _____

6. noware _____

7. somewair _____

8. downstares _____

9. areplanes _____

10. compair _____

11. anywaire _____

12. squair _____

Rabbit Express

Unscramble each word. To solve the riddle, write the circled letters in order on the lines below.

bargain	barn	carpet	charge	chart	garden
parsley	remark	shark	sharply	smart	

1. anigrab ◯ _ _ _ _ _ _
2. seylpar _ _ _ _ _ _ ◯
3. krsah _ ◯ _ _ _
4. tsmra _ ◯ _ _ _
5. rkemra _ _ _ ◯ _ _
6. rndega _ _ _ ◯ _ _
7. pterca _ _ ◯ _ _ _
8. shlypra _ _ _ _ _ ◯ _
9. rtahc _ _ ◯ _ _
10. rabn _ _ ◯ _
11. gechra _ _ _ _ _ ◯

How do rabbits travel?

Answer:

__ __ " __ __ __ __ __ – __ __ __ __ __ __ "

Never Hungry

Why are teddy **bears never** hungry?

Write the word for each clue. To solve the riddle, match the answers to the words in the word bank. Then, write the underlined letters in order on the lines below.

Word Bank
birthd<u>a</u>y
circ<u>l</u>e
c<u>u</u>rve
earl<u>y</u>
<u>f</u>uture
per<u>f</u>ect
purp<u>l</u>e
<u>s</u>earch
<u>s</u>erve
shir<u>t</u>
w<u>a</u>ter
<u>w</u>ork
worl<u>d</u>

1. the day you were born _____

2. a shape with no corners _____

3. what someone does to make a living _____

4. H_2O _____

5. the opposite of *late* _____

6. to start a match in tennis _____

7. to look for something _____

8. another word for *blouse* _____

9. a bend _____

10. without any mistakes _____

11. the opposite of *past* _____

12. the color of red plus blue _____

13. another word for *Earth* _____

Answer: They are ____ ____ ____ ____ ____ ____

____ ____ ____ ____ ____ ____ ____ ____ .

Spelling Puzzler

Write the correct spelling of each word to complete the crossword puzzle.

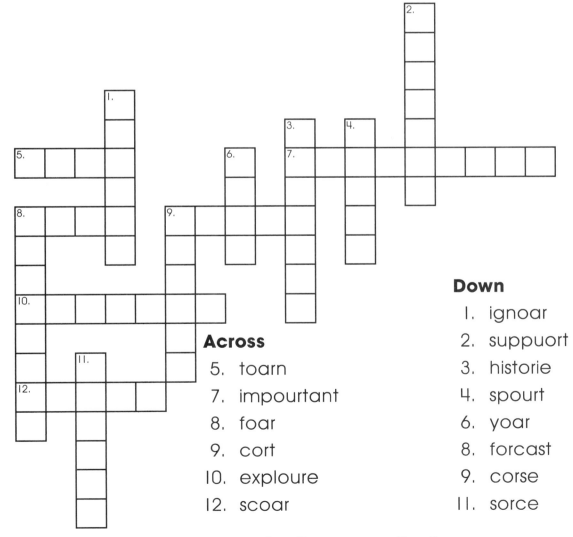

Across

5. toarn
7. impourtant
8. foar
9. cort
10. exploure
12. scoar

Down

1. ignoar
2. suppuort
3. historie
4. spourt
6. yoar
8. forcast
9. corse
11. sorce

"Eggs-actly"!

Draw a line through each word to complete the maze. Letters can connect up, down, left, and right. The first one has been done for you.

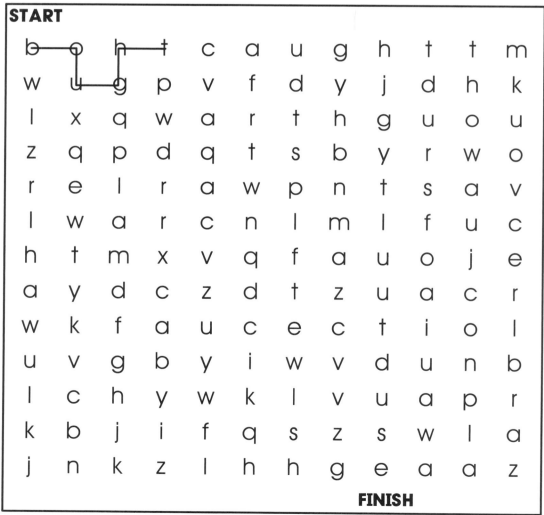

Word list:
- ~~bought~~
- caught
- thought
- straw
- drawn
- crawl
- hawk
- faucet
- fault
- saucer
- caution
- pause

START

b	o	h	t	c	a	u	g	h	t	t	m
w	u	g	p	v	f	d	y	j	d	h	k
l	x	q	w	a	r	t	h	g	u	o	u
z	q	p	d	q	t	s	b	y	r	w	o
r	e	l	r	a	w	p	n	t	s	a	v
l	w	a	r	c	n	l	m	l	f	u	c
h	t	m	x	v	q	f	a	u	o	j	e
a	y	d	c	z	d	t	z	u	a	c	r
w	k	f	a	u	c	e	c	t	i	o	l
u	v	g	b	y	i	w	v	d	u	n	b
l	c	h	y	w	k	l	v	u	a	p	r
k	b	j	i	f	q	s	z	s	w	l	a
j	n	k	z	l	h	h	g	e	a	a	z

FINISH

Enjoy Your Voice

Use the code on the phone keypad to write the word for each clue.

annoy

avoid

coins

enjoy

joyful

loyal

noise

point

rejoice

royalty

1	2 ABC	3 DEF
4 GHI	5 JKL	6 MNO
7 PQRS	8 TUV	9 WXYZ

1. to keep away from   28643   _____

2. to bother someone   26669   _____

3. unwanted sound   66473   _____

4. to have a good time   36569   _____

5. full of happiness   569385   _____

6. faithful   56925   _____

7. to celebrate or to be glad   7356423   _____

8. quarters and pennies   26467   _____

9. the sharp end of a pencil   76468   _____

10. kings and queens   7692589   _____

Ride 'Em Cowboy!

Write a word from the word bank to complete each group of words. Then, match the numbered letters to the numbers below. To solve the riddle, write the letters on the correct lines.

amount	cloudy	couch	drowsy	gown	mouth
plowing	power	shout	sour	south	vowels

1. planting, tilling, ___ ___ ___ ___ ___ ___ ___

2. dress, robe, ___ ___ ___ ___
           3

3. sweet, bitter, ___ ___ ___ ___
              1

4. north, east, ___ ___ ___ ___ ___
           7

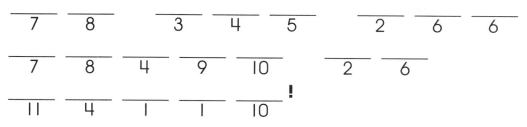

Why did the **cowboy** ride his horse to **town**?

5. chair, coffee table, ___ ___ ___ ___ ___
   11

6. electricity, voltage, ___ ___ ___ ___ ___
            8

7. sum, quantity, ___ ___ ___ ___ ___ ___
      4

8. letters, consonants, ___ ___ ___ ___ ___ ___
      9

9. sunny, rainy, ___ ___ ___ ___ ___ ___
        6

10. scream, yell, ___ ___ ___ ___ ___
     5

11. eyes, nose, ___ ___ ___ ___ ___
         2

12. sleepy, tired, ___ ___ ___ ___ ___ ___
             10

Answer: ___ ___   ___ ___ ___   ___ ___ ___
     7   8   3   4   5   2   6   6

___ ___ ___ ___ ___   ___ ___
  7   8   4   9   10   2   6

___ ___ ___ ___ ___ !
  11   4   1   1   10

Too Long for Two

Color the words that have the long *oo* sound red. Color the remaining words yellow. Then, write the two revealed letters on the lines below.

spoon	jewel	tune	whole	noon	crew	stool
statue	also	include	stood	mood	hour	proof
ruler	goes	prune	family	blue	look	cartoon
hoop	true	moon	kind	cool	tool	soon

Answer:

_____ _____

Hooked on Books

Write the missing letter or letters to complete each short *oo* word, as in *look*. Then, write the word on the line.

1. t _____ k   _____

2. p _____ sh   _____

3. w _____ d   _____

4. sh _____ k   _____

5. p _____ t   _____

6. noteb _____ k   _____

7. f _____ ll   _____

8. w _____ l   _____

9. s _____ gar   _____

10. c _____ shion   _____

11. h _____ k   _____

12. b _____ sh o   _____

Out of Sight

Write the missing letter or letters to complete each word. Then, write the word in the correct column.

1. cha_____e

2. acro_____

3. fan_____y

4. choi_____e

5. _____ereal

6. pa_____age

7. witne_____

8. _____ilent

9. boun_____e

10. cactu_____

11. i_____ue

12. ga_____oline

s	**ss**	**c**
_____	_____	_____
_____	_____	_____
_____	_____	_____
_____	_____	_____

Check Your Clock

Circle each correctly spelled word. To solve the riddle, write the bold letters from the circled words in order on the lines below.

1. kangar**ew**   kan**g**aroo   khanegaroo

2. atti**k**   att**i**ck   atti**c**

3. c**o**ver   **k**over   cov**a**r

4. **b**ekause   be**c**aus   becaus**e**

5. chik**e**n   ch**i**cken   chicki**n**

6. karr**o**t   carro**t**   carot

7. pl**a**stick   plast**i**k   pl**a**stic

8. hoce**y**   ho**c**kee   **h**ockey

9. b**a**con   bak**o**n   ba**c**en

10. **p**iknik   pickni**c**k   pic**n**ic

11. kin**d**   k**h**ind   cined

If your **clock** cannot tell time, what should you do?

Answer: ____ ____ ____ ____   ____ ____

____   ____ ____ ____ ____!

Strange Language

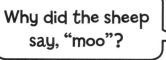

Why did the sheep say, "moo"?

They were learning a new language!

Write *dge*, *g*, *ge*, or *j* to complete each word. Then, write the word on the line.

1. b a __ __ __ _____

2. c h a n __ __ _____

3. __ a c k e t _____

4. g a __ __ __ t _____

5. m e s s a __ __ _____

6. __ u i c e _____

7. __ e n t l e _____

8. b r i __ __ __ _____

9. g a r b a __ __ _____

10. __ e a n s _____

11. __ i a n t _____

12. __ i r a f f e _____

A Herd of Elephants

Write *f, gh*, or *ph* to complete each word. Then, write the word on the line.

1. al_____abet   _____

2. cou_____   _____

3. _____eather   _____

4. lau_____   _____

5. tou_____   _____

6. _____avorite   _____

7. _____otograph   _____

8. ne_____ew   _____

9. ele_____ant   _____

10. enou_____   _____

11. _____riend   _____

12. tele_____one   _____

This and That

Use the code to write each word.

Code:	Z	Y	X	W	V	U	T	S	R	Q	P	O	N
Letter:	a	b	c	d	e	f	g	h	i	j	k	l	m

Code:	M	L	K	J	I	H	G	F	E	D	C	B	A
Letter:	n	o	p	q	r	s	t	u	v	w	x	y	z

1. _____ _____ _____ _____ _____ _____
   L G S V I H

2. _____ _____ _____ _____ _____
   N L F G S

3. _____ _____ _____ _____ _____
   G S V I V

4. _____ _____ _____ _____ _____ _____
   V R G S V I

5. _____ _____ _____ _____ _____ _____ _____
   D V Z G S V I

6. _____ _____ _____ _____ _____
   G V V G S

7. _____ _____ _____ _____ _____
   G S I L D

8. _____ _____ _____ _____ _____ _____
   G S R M T H

9. _____ _____ _____ _____ _____ _____
   T I L D G S

10. _____ _____ _____ _____ _____ _____ _____
    S V Z O G S B

11. _____ _____ _____ _____ _____ _____
    G S L I M H

12. _____ _____ _____ _____ _____
    D R W G S

Rib-Ticklers Spelling

Growing Up

Write the word for each clue. To solve the riddle, write the circled letters in order on the lines below.

ankle	blank
donkey	finger
hungry	kingdom
longer	tangle
young	

Which animal grows the fastest?

1. joint between the foot and the leg ⬭__ __ __ __

2. an animal similar to a horse __ __ __⬭__ __

3. without marks; not written on __ __⬭__ __

4. part of a hand __ __⬭__ __ __

5. needing to eat food __ __ __⬭__ __

6. knot __⬭__ __ __ __

7. the opposite of *shorter* __ __ __ __ __⬭

8. the opposite of *old* __⬭__ __ __

9. land ruled by a king or queen __ __ __ __ __⬭__

Answer:

__ __ __ __ __ __ __ __ because it grows by leaps

and bounds.

Home-Run Spelling

Write the mirror image of each word.

1. offer _____

2. order _____

3. sailor _____

4. sugar _____

5. summer _____

6. dollar _____

7. manner _____

8. writer _____

9. visitor _____

10. author _____

11. grammar _____

12. wonder _____

Word Math

Color the correctly spelled words in each problem. The answers will solve the equation.

1.
pretzel 4   apple 3
pretzle 8   appel 6
+   = 7

2.
rattel 6   riddel 5
rattle 8   riddle 4
+   = 12

3.
puzzle 3   simpel 6
puzzel 4   simple 4
+   = 7

4.
level 9   fable 2
levle 3   fabel 7
+   = 11

5.
camle 7   travel 4
camel 5   travle 5
+   = 9

6.
tabel 2   paddle 2
table 6   paddel 5
+   = 8

Name _____

Get the Picture?

In each group of letters, cross out the first letter and every other letter. Then, write the remaining letters to reveal a word.

1. atbrcedaesfugrhe _____

2. yngahtmugrde _____

3. tpfunrme _____

4. qfwidgtugrbe _____

5. fcguyrhe _____

6. spvahsutjumrne _____

7. kmjihxgtnufrde _____

8. minnbjvucrxe _____

9. pfluotiuurye _____

10. lckrjehagtfudrde _____

11. amsedaisluurje _____

12. zpxivcbtnumrme _____

What can be taken before you even have it?

Your **picture!**

Subtle Riddles

Write the word for each riddle.

climb	comb	crumb	debt	doubt
lamb	limb	numb	thumb	tomb

1. I have teeth but do not chew.
   What am I? _____

2. My mother is a ewe, and my father is a ram.
   What am I? _____

3. I am what you feel when you feel nothing.
   What am I? _____

4. I go hand in hand with your fingers.
   What am I? _____

5. I am what Egyptian mummies call home.
   What am I? _____

6. I am what happens when you owe money.
   What am I? _____

7. I am all that remains when you have eaten your sandwich.
   What am I? _____

8. You are full of me when you lack certainty.
   What am I? _____

9. People, animals, and trees almost always have me.
   What am I? _____

10. I am what a squirrel must do to get home.
    What am I? _____

Hog Foul

Why is it difficult to play basketball with pigs?

They hog the ball!

Unscramble each word.

assign	bought	daughter	design	gnarl	gnat
gnaw	gnome	resign	sign	thought	through

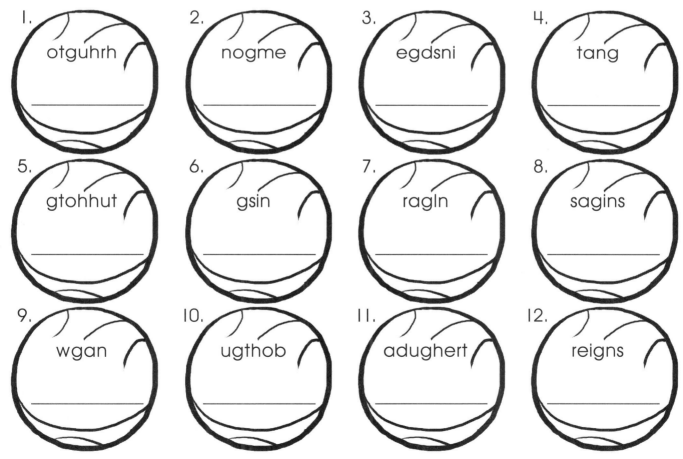

1. otguhrh ____

2. nogme ____

3. egdsni ____

4. tang ____

5. gtohhut ____

6. gsin ____

7. ragln ____

8. sagins ____

9. wgan ____

10. ugthob ____

11. adughert ____

12. reigns ____

A Canoe?

One word in each group is missing a silent *h* or *k*. Add the missing letter and write the correct spelling of the word on the line.

1. spoon, fork, nife   _____

2. nuckle, finger, hand   _____

3. sew, crochet, nit   _____

4. respect, onor, courage   _____

5. truthful, open, onest   _____

6. our, minute, second   _____

7. elbow, nee, ankle   _____

8. stoop, neel, crouch   _____

9. note, music, cord   _____

10. teachers, students, scool _____

11. now, recognize, understand _____

12. tap, bang, nock   _____

An Addressing Problem

Find and color each word in the puzzle. To solve the riddle, write the uncolored letters in order on the lines below.

autumn	calf	chalk	columns	condemn	could	folk
half	salmon	should	talking	walk	would	

s	a	l	m	o	n	a	u	t	u	m	n
A	s	f	o	l	k	b	c	a	l	f	r
c	h	a	w	o	u	l	d	w	a	l	k
h	o	h	h	a	c	o	u	l	d	m	L
a	u	a	c	o	l	u	m	n	s	i	n
l	l	l	c	o	n	d	e	m	n	c	o
k	d	f	l	t	a	l	k	i	n	g	n

I have a Gettysburg address but never lived there. Who am I?

Answer: ____ ____ ____ ____ ____ ____

____ ____ ____ ____ ____ ____

Let's Talk Baseball

Write the word for each clue. To solve the riddle, read down the boxed column.

castle	crutch
fasten	fetch
itch	kitchen
listen	often
patch	scratchy
sketch	soften
stretch	

What did the baseball glove say to the baseball?

1. repair

2. palace

3. draw

4. bring

5. cook's room

6. itchy

7. frequently

8. aid

9. try to hear

10. connect

11. a tickle

12. to calm, soothe

13. spread or expand

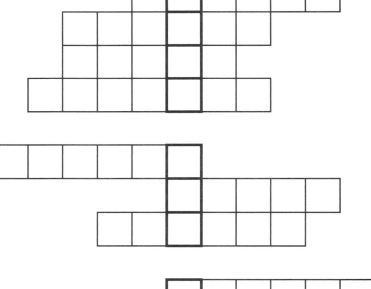

Who's Wrong?

Each word is missing a silent *w*. Write the correct spelling of each word to complete the crossword puzzle.

anser

to

ring

hole

rap

reck

rench

rinkle

rist

rite

reath

What Am I?

Color the words that form the plural with -s blue. Color the words that form the plural with -es green. The picture will solve the riddle.

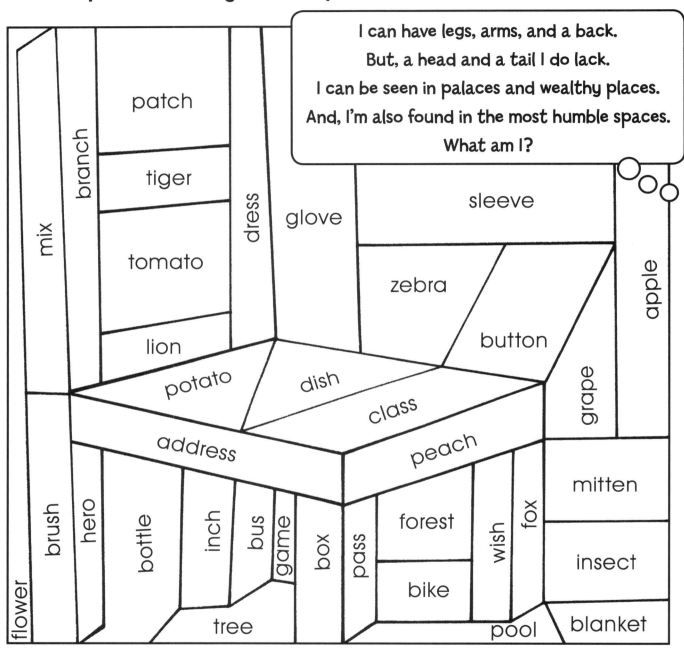

I can have legs, arms, and a back.
But, a head and a tail I do lack.
I can be seen in palaces and wealthy places.
And, I'm also found in the most humble spaces.
What am I?

patch · branch · mix · tiger · tomato · lion · dress · glove · sleeve · zebra · button · apple · grape · potato · dish · class · address · peach · mitten · flower · brush · hero · bottle · inch · bus · game · box · pass · forest · wish · fox · insect · bike · pool · blanket · tree

Answer:

_____

Name _____   ୧୦୭୧

Sunny Side

Circle each correctly spelled word. To solve the riddle, write the underlined letters from the circled words in order on the lines below.

1. batte<u>r</u>ies   bat<u>t</u>erys
2. driv<u>e</u>wayes   dr<u>i</u>veways
3. <u>t</u>urkies   turke<u>y</u>s
4. famili<u>e</u>s   famil<u>y</u>s
5. <u>w</u>orrys   worrie<u>s</u>
6. m<u>o</u>nkeys   monki<u>e</u>s
7. ci<u>t</u>ys   <u>c</u>ities
8. <u>c</u>ountries   count<u>r</u>ys
9. b<u>a</u>bies   ba<u>b</u>ys
10. holi<u>d</u>aies   holiday<u>s</u>
11. m<u>e</u>morys   memor<u>i</u>es
12. story<u>s</u>   st<u>o</u>ries
13. <u>b</u>unnys   bu<u>n</u>nies

> Why can you rely on the sun?

Answer: It always ____ ____ ____ ____ ____

to the ____ ____ ____ ____ ____ ____ ____ ____!

Make Like a Tree

Write the plural form of each word to complete the crossword puzzle.

Across		**Down**	
2. wolf	10. man	1. tooth	6. leaf
6. loaf	12. deer	3. ox	7. foot
8 mouse	14. sheep	4. woman	10. moose
9. shelf	15. goose	5. calf	11. life
	16. wife		13. person

It leaves!

What does a tree do when it is time to go home?

Name That Tune

Complete each compound word with a word part from the word bank. To solve the riddle, write the starred letters in order on the lines below.

bone	corn	end
fly	ground	heart
noon	spoon	tale
vine	watch	yard

Why do **hummingbirds** hum?

1. week ___ ___ ___
   ☆

2. pop ___ ___ ___ ___
                    ☆

3. after ___ ___ ___ ___
              ☆

4. wish ___ ___ ___ ___
   ☆

5. folk ___ ___ ___ ___
   ☆

6. sweet ___ ___ ___ ___ ___
              ☆

7. grape ___ ___ ___ ___
                 ☆

8. wrist ___ ___ ___ ___ ___
   ☆

9. play ___ ___ ___ ___ ___
            ☆

10. barn ___ ___ ___ ___
                 ☆

11. dragon ___ ___ ___
    ☆

12. tea ___ ___ ___ ___ ___
        ☆

Answer: They don't ____ ____ ____ ____

____ ____ ____ ____ ____ ____ ____ .

Peanut Antics

Why did the peanut butter jump into the ocean?

back	fish	foot
home	light	sun

Write the word part from the word bank that can be added to all of the word parts in each list. Then, match the symbols in the words to the symbols below. To solve the riddle, write the correct letters on the lines.

1. __ __ __ __ door

    __ __ __ __ pack

    __ __ __ __ yard
                  △

3. __ __ __ __ print
    ⇨

    __ __ __ __ step

    __ __ __ __ ball

5. __ __ __ light

    __ __ __ shine
    ☆

    __ __ __ flower

2. __ □ __ ⊚ work

    __ __ ● __ made

    __ __ __ __ room

4. gold __ __ __ __

    jelly __ __ __ __
    ○

    star __ ✔ __ __

6. flash __ __ __ ⊚ __

    moon __ __ __ __ __
         ♡

    sun __ __ __ __

Answer: It was looking for

_____!

Double Trouble

Find each word in the puzzle. Color the first syllable of each word orange. Color the second syllable of each word purple.

attic
carrot
coffee
dollar
follow
giggle
hammer
letter
little
pillow
rabbit
sorry
sudden
summer

q	w	e	y	t	r	p	s	o	r	r	y	l	h
z	f	g	j	l	a	i	u	u	y	t	r	k	h
x	r	k	c	v	t	b	m	d	f	g	a	f	a
c	a	r	r	o	t	n	m	k	j	h	s	o	m
r	b	l	c	c	i	q	e	y	i	w	g	l	m
z	b	i	s	q	c	d	r	g	i	g	g	l	e
m	i	t	r	r	c	o	f	f	e	e	o	o	r
m	t	t	n	j	t	l	p	i	l	l	o	w	h
h	t	l	n	r	y	l	m	z	a	q	s	d	g
u	k	e	s	s	g	a	c	v	b	e	s	d	f
k	l	e	t	t	e	r	n	s	u	d	d	e	n

Wealthy Advice

If you want to get rich, why should you stay quiet?

Write the syllables of each word on the lines. Then, circle the last letter of the first syllable in each word. To solve the riddle, write the circled letters in order on the lines below.

1.	escape	es Ⓢ	cape
2.	pilot	_____	_____
3.	silver	_____	_____
4.	result	_____	_____
5.	enter	_____	_____
6.	soccer	_____	_____
7.	even	_____	_____
8.	struggle	_____	_____
9.	odor	_____	_____
10.	velvet	_____	_____
11.	ladder	_____	_____
12.	began	_____	_____
13.	until	_____	_____

Answer: __S__ ____ ____ ____ ____ ____ ____

is ____ ____ ____ ____ ____ ____ .

Rolling Along

What's big and gray and has sixteen wheels?

Circle each word that is correctly divided into syllables. To solve the riddle, write the underlined letters from the circled words in order on the lines below.

1. be/tween
   bet/ween

2. comp/lete
   com/plete

3. din/ner
   dinn/er

4. peo/ple
   peop/le

5. he/ro
   her/o

6. in/stead
   ins/tead

7. coun/try
   countr/y

8. pret/ty
   prett/y

9. sist/er
   sis/ter

10. back/pack
    backp/ack

11. grape/vine
    grap/evine

12. wi/thout
    with/out

13. bet/ter
    bett/er

14. su/mmer
    sum/mer

Answer: an ____ ____ ____ ____ ____ ____ ____ ____

on ____ ____ ____ ____ ____ ____

Humorous Homophones

Circle each misspelled homophone and write the correct spelling.

bear   buy   coral   flew   horse   pair   patients   scents   sea   tail

1. Do grizzly bears wear shoes?
   No, they have "beare" feet.

   _____

2. Why couldn't the pony talk?
   He was a little "hoorse."

   _____

3. Where can you hear music in the ocean?
   At the "corale" reef. _____

4. How do salespeople say farewell?
   "Good-buye!" _____

5. Do pilots get colds?
   No, they get the "fleew."

   _____

6. What did the man say when he saw the ocean for the first time?
   Long time, no "seaa." _____

7. What kind of trees are always with a friend?
   "Piar" trees are always with a friend. _____

8. Why will no one borrow money from a skunk?
   Skunks give out bad "skents."

   _____

9. What kind of story is "The Three Little Pigs"?
   It is a pig "taile." _____

10. Why are doctors so calm?
    They have a lot of "paytients."

    _____

More Humorous Homophones

Write a homophone for each underlined word.

1. What is the smartest part of a person's face?
   A "knows" is the smartest part of the face. _____

2. What type of gardens do bakers plant?
   Bakers plant "flour" gardens. _____

3. When are children like pieces of wood?
   When they are a little "board." _____

4. What do frogs wear on their feet?
   They wear "open-toad" shoes. _____

5. Why was the chicken upset?
   She was in a "fowl" mood. _____

6. What insect runs away from everything?
   A "flee" runs away from
   everything. _____

7. What kind of tree has the most hair?
   A "fur" tree has the most
   hair. _____

8. Why did the boy put a shower cap on
   a rabbit?
   He didn't want her "hare" to get
   wet. _____

Name _____

A Dress Is a Dress

Find and color each word in the puzzle. To solve the riddle, write the uncolored letters in order on the lines below.

a	e	n	t	r	a	n	c	e	p	n	c
w	a	p	r	e	s	e	n	t	r	r	o
o	c	r	r	o	u	t	e	d	o	e	n
u	o	e	o	b	j	e	c	t	j	c	f
n	n	b	l	d	t	e	a	r	e	o	l
d	d	e	e	s	e	w	e	r	c	r	i
b	u	l	a	b	a	s	s	r	t	d	c
o	c	e	d	c	o	n	t	e	n	t	t
w	t	p	r	o	d	u	c	e	s	o	w
s	d	e	s	e	r	t	r	e	a	d	s
c	o	n	t	r	a	c	t	w	i	n	d
d	o	v	e	i	n	c	r	e	a	s	e

bass	bow
conduct	conflict
content	contract
desert	dove
entrance	increase
lead	object
present	produce
project	read
rebel	record
route	sewer
sow	tear
wind	wound

What kind of dress do you never wear?

Answer:

_____ " _____ _____ _____ _____ _____ _____ _____ "

Putting Down Roots

Underline the root word of each word. Then, write the word from the word bank that has the same root word.

autograph	boxed	chilly	downtown	fortunate
heater	joyous	review	tricycle	walker

1. walking _____

2. boxes _____

3. reheat _____

4. bicycle _____

5. joyful _____

6. chilled _____

7. automobile _____

8. midtown _____

9. preview _____

10. misfortune _____

Paying the Bill

Circle the words in the puzzle.

action
actor
react
astronaut
asteroid
image
imagine
local
locate
location
minus
minute

a	o	m	i	n	u	s	t	i	n	g
b	v	k	a	j	s	d	r	m	m	l
l	h	a	c	t	i	o	n	a	i	o
o	j	l	t	k	a	i	c	g	n	c
c	z	q	o	l	x	m	w	e	u	a
a	s	t	r	o	n	a	u	t	t	t
t	r	e	a	c	t	g	y	q	e	i
e	r	t	u	a	l	i	o	i	k	o
q	u	k	j	l	z	n	c	b	v	n
r	t	g	a	s	t	e	r	o	i	d

Eyesight Insight

Add the prefix *dis-*, *non-*, or *un-* to each word to make its opposite. To solve the riddle, write the circled letters in order on the lines below.

1. approve   __ __ __ __ __ __ ◯ __ __ __

2. affected   __ __ ◯ __ __ __ __ __ __ __

3. obey   __ __ __ ◯ __ __ __

4. verbal   __ __ __ __ __ __ ◯ __ __

5. fiction   __ __ __ __ ◯ __ __ __ __

6. limited   __ __ __ __ __ __ ◯ __ __

7. usual   __ __ ◯ __ __ __ __

8. agree   __ __ __ ◯ __ __ __

9. lucky   __ __ ◯ __ __ __

10. paid   __ __ ◯ __ __

11. sense   __ __ ◯ __ __ __ __

12. honest   __ ◯ __ __ __ __ __

13. true   __ __ __ __ ◯ __

14. stop   __ __ ◯ __ __

How do you know that carrots are good for your eyesight?

Answer: ____ ____ ____ ____ ____ ____ ____ don't

wear ____ ____ ____ ____ ____ ____ !

Underwater Mystery

Unscramble each word. Then, add a prefix and write the new word on the line.

> over-   sub-   under-

1. nurt   _____   _____

2. tilet   _____   _____

3. ywa   _____   _____

4. ipad   _____   _____

5. taewr   _____   _____

6. leni   _____   _____

7. eplse   _____   _____

8. ahte   _____   _____

9. trcta   _____   _____

10. taoc   _____   _____

Searching for Answers

Use the code to write each word.

Code:	M	N	O	P	Q	R	S	T	U	V	W	X	Y
Letter:	a	b	c	d	e	f	g	h	i	j	k	l	m

Code:	Z	A	B	C	D	E	F	G	H	I	J	K	L
Letter:	n	o	p	q	r	s	t	u	v	w	x	y	z

1. BDQOMGFUAZ _____

2. RADQMDY _____

3. BDAOQQP _____

4. BDAPGOQ _____

5. BDQTQMF _____

6. RADQTQMP _____

7. BDASDQEE _____

8. BDQEOTAAX _____

9. BDQHUQI _____

10. RADQOMEF _____

11. RADQIADP _____

12. BDAOXMUY _____

Coordinate the Coordinates

Use the grid to write each word part. Then, write the word on the line.

	A	B	C	D	E	F	G	H	I	J	K	L
9			g						l			
8						o					c	
7				t								
6	v						e		n			s
5			r									
4					a					u		
3		m						d				y
2				i						b		
1						p						

1. mis ___ ___ ___ _____
   (J,4) (L,6) (G,6)

2. mis ___ ___ ___ ___ _____
   (I,9) (G,6) (E,4) (H,3)

3. con ___ ___ ___ ___ ___ ___ ___ _____
   (A,6) (G,6) (I,6) (D,7) (D,2) (F,8) (I,6)

4. con ___ ___ ___ ___ _____
   (D,7) (G,6) (L,6) (D,7)

5. com ___ ___ ___ ___ ___ ___ _____
   (F,1) (G,6) (D,7) (D,2) (I,6) (C,9)

6. mis ___ ___ ___ ___ ___ _____
   (F,1) (I,9) (E,4) (K,8) (G,6)

7. con ___ ___ ___ ___ ___ _____
   (A,6) (D,2) (I,6) (K,8) (G,6)

8. anti ___ ___ ___ ___ _____
   (H,3) (F,8) (D,7) (G,6)

9. con ___ ___ ___ ___ ___ ___ ___ _____
   (D,7) (C,5) (D,2) (J,2) (J,4) (D,7) (G,6)

10. mis ___ ___ ___ ___ ___ _____
    (F,1) (C,5) (D,2) (I,6) (D,7)

Autumn Colors

Write a prefix to complete each word. Then, write the word on the line. Use the key to color the words.

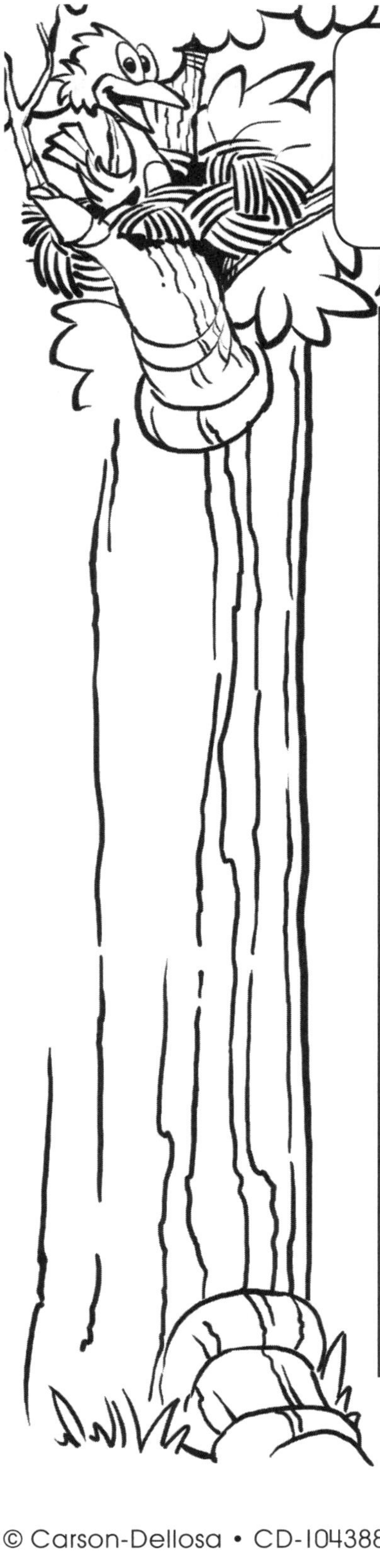

ex- words = red

mid- words = yellow

re- words = orange

_____night _____	_____spond _____	_____plain _____
_____move _____	_____plore _____	_____way _____
_____peat _____	_____air _____	_____tend _____
_____cuse _____	_____week _____	_____ply _____
_____day _____	_____play _____	_____ternal _____

How Many?

Complete the table. Then, use the table to complete the crossword puzzle.

The prefix means:	The word is:
one	_____form
two	_____cycle
three	_____pod
five	_____agon
six	_____agon
eight	_____opus
ten	_____ade
one hundred	_____pede

Heavy Objects

Write a pair of antonyms using each root word.

		-ful	-less
1.	care	_____	_____
2.	color	_____	_____
3.	doubt	_____	_____
4.	fear	_____	_____
5.	flavor	_____	_____
6.	help	_____	_____
7.	hope	_____	_____
8.	meaning	_____	_____
9.	pain	_____	_____
10.	power	_____	_____
11.	thank	_____	_____
12.	thought	_____	_____

Special Species

Unscramble each word. To solve the riddle, write the circled letters in order on the lines below.

1. dalyi __ (__) __ __ __

2. floram __ __ __ __ __ (__)

3. lolyws __ __ __ (__) __ __

4. anssloea __ __ __ __ __ (__) __

5. sojouy __ (__) __ __ __ __

6. uvsnireal __ __ __ __ __ (__) __ __

7. ueomnurs __ __ __ __ __ __ (__) __

8. lspimy __ __ (__) __ __ __

9. msonuroe __ __ __ __ (__) __ __ __

10. diagitl __ __ (__) __ __ __ __

11. trylefcep __ __ __ __ __ __ (__) __ __

12. uensvor (__) __ __ __ __ __ __

13. nlusddye __ __ (__) __ __ __ __ __

daily
digital
enormous
formal
joyous
nervous
numerous
perfectly
seasonal
simply
slowly
suddenly
universal

Why can't a leopard hide?

Answer: He is __ __ __ __ __ __ __ __ __ __ __ __!

Helmet Head

Draw a line through the correctly spelled words to help the cyclist find his helmet.

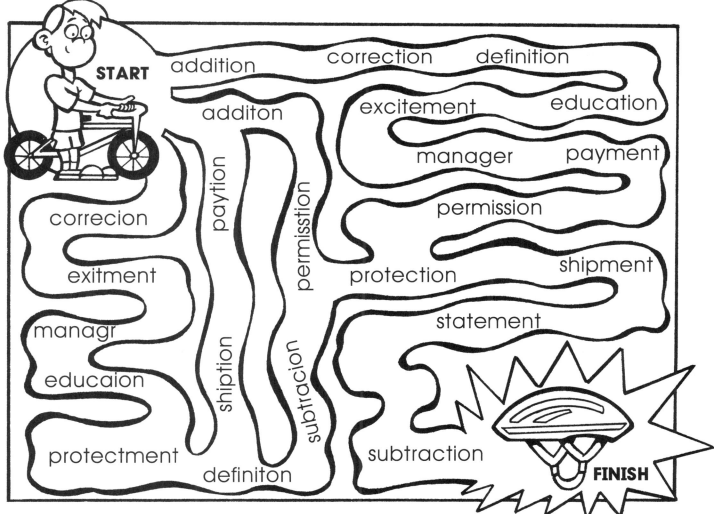

Adding Suffixes

Complete the crossword puzzle. Each word will have a suffix from the word bank.

-en

-(i)ze

-(i)fy

Across

2. to make simple
4. to make an apology
6. to make social
7. to increase in strength
10. to make a criticism
11. to make familiar
12. to make deep

Down

1. when something is the color of gold
3. to make personal
5. to prove something is just
8. to make bright
9. to make final

Name ______________________________

Suffix Search

Circle the 18 words in the puzzle. Then, write the words on the lines.

activeadorableartisticcreativeelectricalfantastichistoricpayablepossiblereadabletalkativewashablescenicfranticpassivemajesticoffensiveterrific

More but Less

In each group of letters, cross out the first letter and every other letter. Then, write the remaining letters to reveal a word.

1. aspeorqisodufs   _____

2. lsktjahrgrfy   _____

3. qswcerfavtkchhly   _____

4. mgnobobdvncexszs   _____

5. pciouzty   _____

6. zgxrcevabtvnmelsks   _____

7. hsjakdlnpeosus   _____

8. rctltuymisoinnkelsjs   _____

9. vcblnelakrklwy   _____

10. pwoillkdjehrgnfevscs   _____

11. aksidnjdkniepsrs   _____

12. lfkrjohsutry   _____

What's the Answer?

Why did Ana have trouble with her spelling tests?

The teacher kept changing the spelling words!

Draw an X on each misspelled word and write the correct spelling.

1.	dryed	drying
2.	smiled	smilling
3.	turned	turnning
4.	grabed	grabbing
5.	carried	carring
6.	cliped	clipping
7.	studyed	studying
8.	stopped	stoping
9.	hoopped	hoping
10.	cared	carring
11.	hired	hirring
12.	caled	calling

Today's Spelling

Write the -*ing* and -*ed* forms of each verb.

	-ing	-ed
1. drop	_____	_____
2. rub	_____	_____
3. stripe	_____	_____
4. hop	_____	_____
5. dance	_____	_____
6. cause	_____	_____
7. pop	_____	_____
8. use	_____	_____
9. drip	_____	_____
10. bake	_____	_____
11. drag	_____	_____
12. time	_____	_____

Finding the Largers

Who is **largest**:
Mr. **Larger**,
Mrs. **Larger**,
or
their baby?

The baby is a little **Larger**.

Draw an X on each misspelled word and write the correct spelling.

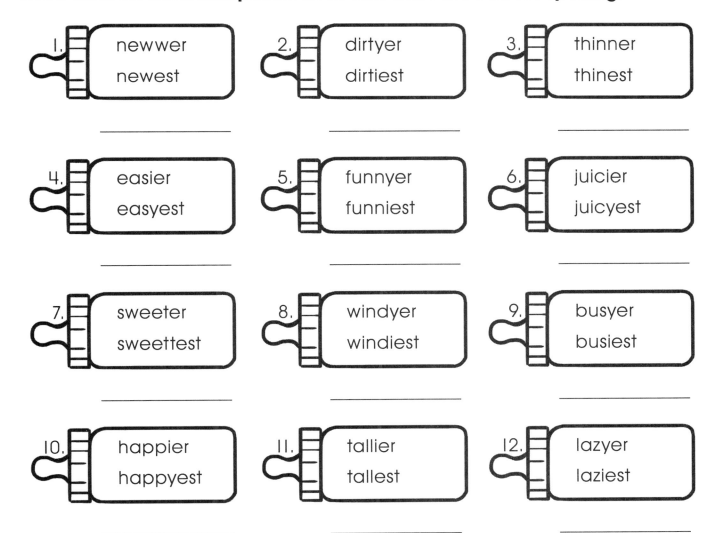

1. newwer
   newest
   _____

2. dirtyer
   dirtiest
   _____

3. thinner
   thinest
   _____

4. easier
   easyest
   _____

5. funnyer
   funniest
   _____

6. juicier
   juicyest
   _____

7. sweeter
   sweettest
   _____

8. windyer
   windiest
   _____

9. busyer
   busiest
   _____

10. happier
    happyest
    _____

11. tallier
    tallest
    _____

12. lazyer
    laziest
    _____

 Rib-Ticklers Spelling

Drumbeats

Write the -*er* and -*est* forms of each adjective.

	-er	-est
1. bold	_____	_____
2. deep	_____	_____
3. hard	_____	_____
4. nice	_____	_____
5. light	_____	_____
6. near	_____	_____
7. quick	_____	_____
8. close	_____	_____
9. old	_____	_____
10. large	_____	_____
11. brave	_____	_____
12. high	_____	_____

The Long and Short of It

Write the correct word for each abbreviation.

Word Bank
Apartment
Avenue
Doctor
February
foot
Friday
inch
kilometer
Post Office
Road
Street
Tuesday

1. Apt. _____

2. ft. _____

3. St. _____

4. Fri. _____

5. Rd. _____

6. Ave. _____

7. km _____

8. Tues. _____

9. in. _____

10. Feb. _____

11. Dr. _____

12. PO _____

Know Your Numbers

Write the word for each number to complete the crossword puzzle.

Down

2. 13
3. 70
6. 10th
7. 12th
8. 90

Across

1. 9th
4. 4th
5. 17
6. 20
9. 100
10. 8th

Awesome Apostrophes

Write the contraction for each pair of words. Then, match the symbols in the answers to the symbols below. To solve the riddle, write the correct letters on the lines.

1. they are ____ ____ ____ ____ ' ____ ____
   ◇

2. do not ____ ____ ____ ' ____
   ⊠

3. let us ____ ____ ____ ' ____
   ☺

4. is not ____ ____ ____ ' ____
   ◉

5. does not ____ ____ ____ ____ ____ ' ____
   ▯   ○

6. will not ____ ____ ____ ' ____
   △

7. are not ____ ____ ____ ____ ' ____
   ☆

Answer: So he'd get a

A Big Splash

Use the code to write each word.

Code:	M	N	O	P	Q	R	S	T	U	V	W	X	Y
Letter:	a	b	c	d	e	f	g	h	i	j	k	l	m

Code:	Z	A	B	C	D	E	F	G	H	I	J	K	L
Letter:	n	o	p	q	r	s	t	u	v	w	x	y	z

1. FTQUD   _____

2. OMZZAF   _____

3. ITUOT   _____

4. ABQZ   _____

5. BXQMEQ   _____

6. RDUQZP   _____

7. FAPMK   _____

8. PAQE   _____

9. YGOT   _____

10. AFTQD   _____

11. NQOMGEQ   _____

12. NAFT   _____

Where do race cars go swimming?

In a carpool!

The Perfect Pencil

Write the word for each clue. To solve the riddle, write the circled letters in order on the lines below.

1. typically; normally _ ( ) _ ( ) _ _ _

2. between; in the midst _ ( ) _ _ _

3. unique _ _ ( ) _ _ _

4. total; whole _ _ ( ) _ _ _ _ _

5. transport _ _ ( ) _ _

6. tough ( ) ( ) _ _ _ _

7. in the direction of _ _ _ ( ) _ _

8. the opposite of *give* ( ) ( ) _ _

9. good; _ _ ( ) _ _ _ ; best

10. raise; produce _ _ _ ( )

11. urban area _ ( ) _ _

12. before *twice* _ _ ( ) ( )

among
better
bring
city
complete
grow
keep
once
special
strong
toward
usually

Why did the pencil have an eraser at each end?

Answer: in case it makes the __ __ __ __

__ __ __ __ __ __ __ __ __ __

Punny Titles

**Circle the misspelled word in each title. Then, write the correct spelling
on the line.**

1. *Gitting to the Beach* by C. Shore _____

2. *My Favurite Sleepwear* by P. Jays _____

3. *Wuld Have Been a Great Baseball Player* by Kent Hitt _____

4. *I'm Verry Hungry* by E. Tunuff _____

5. *I Woont to Help* by Abel N. Willin _____

6. *How to Mayk Honey* by B. A. Beaman _____

7. *Morening Radio* by A. M. Effem _____

8. *And Nou the Following Announcements* by P. A. Sistem _____

9. *Let's Playe Billiards* by A. Q. Ball _____

10. *Life Befour Cars* by A. Orson Buggy _____

11. *Nuts Abot You!* by Ella Fant _____

12. *Thay Are Not Cows* by M. R. Horses _____

A Huge Problem

Write the antonym for each clue. To solve the riddle, write the circled letters in order on the lines below.

against	came
every	friend
making	remember
separate	special
young	

> When does a mouse weigh the same as an elephant?

1. in favor of ___ ___ ___ ___ (___) ___

2. went (___) ___ ___ ___

3. together ___ ___ ___ (___) ___ ___ ___

4. ordinary ___ ___ ___ ___ ___ (___)

5. forget ___ (___) ___ ___ (___) ___ ___

6. none ___ ___ ___ (___)

7. old ___ (___) ___ ___ ___

8. destroying ___ ___ (___) ___ ___ ___

9. enemy ___ ___ ___ (___) (___) ___

Answer:

when the ___ ___ ___ ___ ___ is ___ ___ ___ ___ ___ ___

Private Eye

Use the code to write each word.

Code:	M	N	O	P	Q	R	S	T	U	V	W	X	Y
Letter:	a	b	c	d	e	f	g	h	i	j	k	l	m

Code:	Z	A	B	C	D	E	F	G	H	I	J	K	L
Letter:	n	o	p	q	r	s	t	u	v	w	x	y	z

1. TQMDP _____

2. MITUXQ _____

3. YUSTF _____

4. QJOQBF _____

5. OQZFGDK _____

6. XUNDMDK _____

7. RUZMXXK _____

8. BADFDMUF _____

9. IDAFQ _____

10. YMOTUZQ _____

11. OMYQDM _____

12. UZFA _____

Page 5
1. ranch; 2. fabric; 3. plant; 4. snack;
5. past; 6. facts; 7. stamp; 8. glass;
9. after; a banana split

Page 6
1. fresh; 2. spelling; 3. hedge; 4. pledge;
5. healthy; 6. extra; 7. never; 8. feather;
9. breakfast; eggplants

Page 7
1. package; 2. middle; 3. prints; 4. myth;
5. pinch; 6. typical; 7. fiction; 8. building;
9. village; 10. gym; 11. built; 12. wreckage

Page 8
1. chomp; 2. wash; 3. strong; 4. pocket;
5. novel; 6. watch; 7. solve; 8. drop; 9. frog;
10. shock; 11. robin; 12. problem;

Page 9
1. puppet; 2. bucket; 3. skunk; 4. front;
5. brother; 6. funny; 7. nothing; 8. slug;
a belly button

Page 10
1. steak, stake; 2. raise, rays (raze); 3. way,
weigh (whey); 4. wait, weight; 5. ate, eight;
6. waist, waste; 7. pain, pane; 8. grate, great;
9. brake, break; 10. pail, pale

Page 11
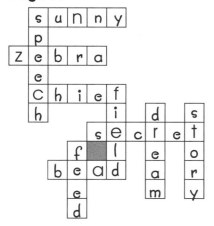

Page 12
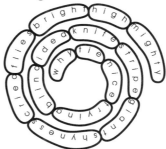

Page 13
1. float; 2. goes; 3. coach; 4. almost;
5. thrown; 6. poem; 7. ocean; 8. roses;
9. alone; 10. shallow; a scarecrow

Page 14
1. spare; 2. everywhere; 3. repair; 4. declare;
5. upstairs; 6. nowhere; 7. somewhere;
8. downstairs; 9. airplanes; 10. compare;
11. anywhere; 12. square

Page 15
1. bargain; 2. parsley; 3. shark; 4. smart;
5. remark; 6. garden; 7. carpet; 8. sharply;
9. chart; 10. barn; 11. charge; by "hare-plane"

Page 16
1. birthday; 2. circle; 3. work; 4. water;
5. early; 6. serve; 7. search; 8. shirt; 9. curve;
10. perfect; 11. future; 12. purple; 13. world;
They are always stuffed.

Page 17

9. Down: course or coarse

Page 18

START

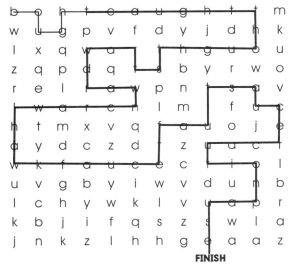

FINISH

Page 19
1. avoid; 2. annoy; 3. noise; 4. enjoy;
5. joyful; 6. loyal; 7. rejoice; 8. coins;
9. point; 10. royalty

Page 20
1. plowing; 2. gown; 3. sour; 4. south;
5. couch; 6. power; 7. amount;
8. vowels; 9. cloudy; 10. shout;
11. mouth; 12. drowsy; He was too heavy
to carry!

Page 21
These words should be colored red: jewel,
crew, statue, include, mood, proof, ruler,
prune, blue, cartoon, true, tool, spoon, tune,
moon, hoop, stool, cool, soon, noon; These
words should be colored yellow: whole, also,
stood, hour, goes, family, look, kind; oo

Page 22
1. took; 2. push; 3. wood; 4. shook;
5. put; 6. notebook; 7. full; 8. wool;
9. sugar; 10. cushion; 11. hook; 12. bush

Page 23
s words: chase, silent, cactus, gasoline;
ss words: across, passage, witness, issue;
c words: fancy, choice, cereal, bounce

Page 24
1. kangaroo; 2. attic; 3. cover;
4. because; 5. chicken; 6. carrot;
7. plastic; 8. hockey; 9. bacon;
10. picnic; 11. kind; Give it a hand!

Page 25
1. badge; 2. change; 3. jacket;
4. gadget; 5. message; 6. juice;
7. gentle; 8. bridge; 9. garbage;
10. jeans; 11. giant; 12. giraffe

Page 26
1. alphabet; 2. cough; 3. feather;
4. laugh; 5. tough; 6. favorite;
7. photograph; 8. nephew; 9. elephant;
10. enough; 11. friend; 12. telephone

Page 27
1. others; 2. mouth; 3. there; 4. either;
5. weather; 6. teeth; 7. throw; 8. things;
9. growth; 10. healthy; 11. thorns;
12. width

Page 28
1. ankle; 2. donkey; 3. blank; 4. finger;
5. hungry; 6. tangle; 7. longer;
8. young; 9. kingdom; A kangaroo
because it grows by leaps and bounds.

Page 29
1. offer; 2. order; 3. sailor; 4. sugar;
5. summer; 6. dollar; 7. manner;
8. writer; 9. visitor; 10. author;
11. grammar; 12. wonder

Page 30
1. pretzel, apple; 2. rattle, riddle;
3. puzzle, simple; 4. level, fable;
5. camel, travel; 6. table, paddle

Page 31
1. treasure; 2. nature; 3. pure; 4. figure;
5. cure; 6. pasture; 7. mixture; 8. injure;
9. future; 10. creature; 11. measure;
12. picture

Page 32
1. comb; 2. lamb; 3. numb; 4. thumb;
5. tomb; 6. debt; 7. crumb; 8. doubt;
9. limb; 10. climb

Page 33
1. through; 2. gnome; 3. design;
4. gnat; 5. thought; 6. sign; 7. gnarl;
8. assign; 9. gnaw; 10. bought;
11. daughter; 12. resign

Page 34
1. knife; 2. knuckle; 3. knit; 4. honor;
5. honest; 6. hour; 7. knee; 8. kneel;
9. chord; 10. school; 11. know; 12. knock

Page 35
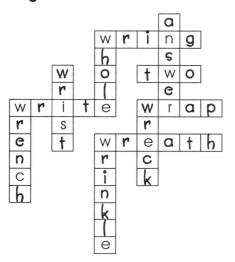

Abraham Lincoln

Page 36
1. patch; 2. castle; 3. sketch; 4. fetch;
5. kitchen; 6. scratchy; 7. often;
8. crutch; 9. listen; 10. fasten; 11. itch;
12. soften; 13. stretch; catch you later

Page 37

Page 38
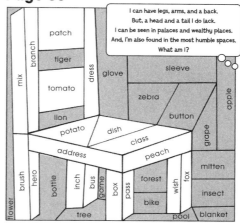

These words should be colored blue: tiger, glove, sleeve, lion, zebra, button, grape, apple, flower, bottle, game, forest, mitten, tree, bike, insect, pool, blanket; These words should be colored green: patch, branch, mix, tomato, dress, potato, dish, class, address, peach, brush, hero, inch, bus, box, pass, wish, fox.; a chair

Page 39
1. batteries; 2. driveways; 3. turkeys;
4. families; 5. worries; 6. monkeys;
7. cities; 8. countries; 9. babies;
10. holidays; 11. memories; 12. stories;
13. bunnies; It always rises to the occasion!

Page 40
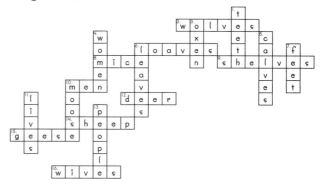

Page 41
1. weekend; 2. popcorn; 3. afternoon;
4. wishbone; 5. folktale; 6. sweetheart;
7. grapevine; 8. wristwatch; 9. playground;
10. barnyard; 11. dragonfly; 12. teaspoon;
They don't know the words.

Page 42

1. back; 2. home; 3. foot; 4. fish; 5. sun;
6. light; It was looking for some jellyfish!

Page 43

q	w	e	y	t	r	p	s	o	r	r	y	l	h
z	f	g	j	l	a	i	u	u	y	t	r	k	h
x	r	k	c	v	t	b	m	d	f	g	a	f	a
c	a	r	r	o	t	n	m	k	j	h	s	o	m
r	b	l	c	c	i	q	e	y	i	w	g	l	m
z	b	l	s	q	c	d	r	g	i	g	g	l	e
m	i	t	r	r	c	o	f	f	e	e	o	o	r
m	t	t	n	j	t	l	p	i	l	l	o	w	h
h	t	l	n	r	y	i	m	z	a	q	s	d	g
u	k	e	s	s	g	a	c	v	b	e	s	d	f
k	l	e	t	t	e	r	n	s	u	d	d	e	n

Page 44

1. es/cape; 2. pi/lot; 3. sil/ver; 4. re/sult;
5. en/ter; 6. soc/cer; 7. e/ven; 8. strug/gle;
9. o/dor; 10. vel/vet; 11. lad/der;
12. be/gan; 13. un/til; Silence is golden.

Page 45

1. be/tween; 2. com/plete; 3. din/ner;
4. peo/ple; 5. he/ro; 6. in/stead;
7. coun/try; 8. pret/ty; 9. sis/ter;
10. back/pack; 11. grape/vine;
12. with/out; 13. bet/ter; 14. sum/mer;
an elephant on skates

Page 46

1. bear; 2. horse; 3. coral; 4. buy; 5. flew; 6 sea;
7. pair; 8. scents; 9. tail; 10. patients

Page 47

1. nose; 2. flower; 3. bored; 4. toed;
5. foul; 6. flea; 7. fir; 8. hair

Page 48

a	e	n	t	r	a	n	c	e	p	n	c
w	a	p	r	e	s	e	n	t	r	r	o
o	c	r	r	o	u	t	e	d	o	e	n
u	o	e	o	b	j	e	c	t	j	c	f
n	n	b	l	d	t	e	a	r	e	o	l
d	d	e	e	s	e	w	e	r	c	r	i
b	u	l	a	b	a	s	s	r	t	d	c
o	c	e	d	c	o	n	t	e	n	t	t
w	t	p	r	o	d	u	c	e	s	o	w
s	d	e	s	e	r	t	r	e	a	d	s
c	o	n	t	r	a	c	t	w	i	n	d
d	o	v	e	i	n	c	r	e	a	s	e

an "address"

Page 49

1. <u>walk</u>, walker; 2. <u>box</u>, boxed; 3. <u>heat</u>, heater;
4. <u>cycle</u>, tricycle; 5. <u>joy</u>, joyous; 6. <u>chill</u>, chilly;
7. <u>auto</u>, autograph; 8. <u>town</u>, downtown;
9. <u>view</u>, review; 10. <u>fortune</u>, fortunate

Page 50

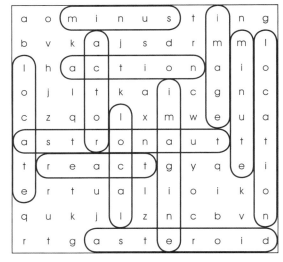

Page 51

1. disapprove; 2. unaffected;
3. disobey; 4. nonverbal; 5. nonfiction;
6. unlimited; 7. unusual; 8. disagree;
9. unlucky; 10. unpaid; 11. nonsense;
12. dishonest; 13. untrue; 14. nonstop;
Rabbits don't wear glasses!

Page 52

1. turn, overturn; 2. title, subtitle; 3. way, subway or underway; 4. paid, underpaid or overpaid; 5. water, underwater; 6. line, underline; 7. sleep, oversleep; 8. heat, overheat; 9. tract, subtract; 10. coat, overcoat or undercoat

Page 53

1. precaution; 2. forearm; 3. proceed; 4. produce; 5. preheat; 6. forehead; 7. progress; 8. preschool; 9. preview; 10. forecast; 11. foreword; 12. proclaim

Page 54

1. use, misuse; 2. lead, mislead; 3. vention, convention; 4. test, contest; 5. peting, competing; 6. place, misplace; 7. vince, convince; 8. dote, antidote; 9. tribute, contribute; 10. print, misprint

Page 55

midnight, respond, explain, remove, explore, midway, repeat, midair, extend, excuse (recuse), midweek, reply, midday, replay, external; These words should be colored red: explain, explore, extend, excuse, external; These words should be colored orange: respond, remove, repeat, (recuse), reply, replay; These words should be colored yellow: midnight, midway, midair, midweek, midday

Page 56

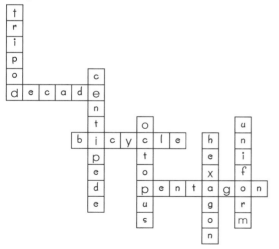

Page 57

1. careful, careless; 2. colorful, colorless; 3. doubtful, doubtless; 4. fearful, fearless; 5. flavorful, flavorless; 6. helpful, helpless; 7. hopeful, hopeless; 8. meaningful, meaningless; 9. painful, painless; 10. powerful, powerless; 11. thankful, thankless; 12. thoughtful, thoughtless

Page 58

1. daily; 2. formal; 3. slowly; 4. seasonal; 5. joyous; 6. universal; 7. numerous; 8. simply; 9. enormous; 10. digital; 11. perfectly; 12. nervous; 13. suddenly; He is always spotted!

Page 59

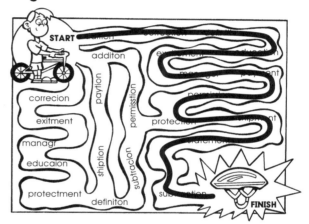

Page 60

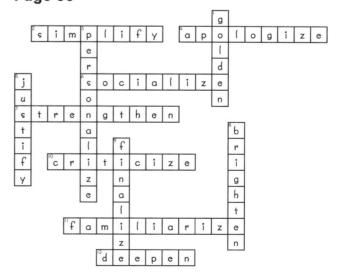

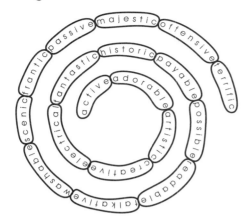 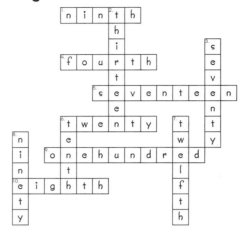
Page 61

Page 68

Page 62
1. serious; 2. starry; 3. scratchy;
4. goodness; 5. cozy; 6. greatness;
7. sadness; 8. clumsiness; 9. clearly;
10. wilderness; 11. kindness; 12. frosty

Page 63
1. dried; 2. smiling; 3. turning; 4. grabbed;
5. carrying; 6. clipped; 7. studied; 8. stopping;
9. hoped; 10. caring; 11. hiring; 12. called

Page 64
1. dropping, dropped; 2. rubbing, rubbed;
3. striping, striped; 4. hopping, hopped;
5. dancing, danced; 6. causing, caused;
7. popping, popped; 8. using, used;
9. dripping, dripped; 10. baking, baked;
11. dragging, dragged; 12. timing, timed

Page 65
1. newer; 2. dirtier; 3. thinnest; 4. easiest;
5. funnier; 6. juiciest; 7. sweetest; 8. windier;
9. busier; 10. happiest; 11. taller; 12. lazier

Page 66
1. bolder, boldest; 2. deeper, deepest;
3. harder, hardest; 4. nicer, nicest; 5. lighter,
lightest; 6. nearer, nearest; 7. quicker,
quickest; 8. closer, closest; 9. older, oldest;
10. larger, largest; 11. braver, bravest;
12. higher, highest

Page 67
1. Apartment; 2. foot; 3. Street;
4. Friday; 5. Road; 6. Avenue; 7. kilometer;
8. Tuesday; 9. inch; 10. February;
11. Doctor; 12. Post Office

Page 69
1. they're; 2. don't; 3. let's; 4. isn't; 5. doesn't;
6. won't; 7. aren't; So he'd get a new story.

Page 70
1. their; 2. cannot; 3. which; 4. open;
5. please; 6. friend; 7. today; 8. does; 9. much;
10. other; 11. because; 12. both

Page 71
1. usually; 2. among; 3. special; 4. complete;
5. bring; 6. strong; 7. toward; 8. keep; 9. better;
10. grow; 11. city; 12. once; in case it makes
the same mistake twice

Page 72
1. Getting; 2. Favorite; 3. Would; 4. Very;
5. Want; 6. Make; 7. Morning; 8. Now; 9. Play;
10. Before; 11. About; 12. They

Page 73
1. against; 2. came; 3. separate; 4. special;
5. remember; 6. every; 7. young; 8. making;
9. friend; when the scale is broken

Page 74
1. heard; 2. awhile; 3. might; 4. except;
5. century; 6. library; 7. finally; 8. portrait;
9. wrote; 10. machine; 11. camera; 12. into